DINOSAUR
ADVENTURES

The Jurassic Period

Ashley Lee

VANCOUVER, B.C.

WWW.ENGAGEBOOKS.COM

The Jurassic Period Level 1
Lee, Ashley 1995
Text © 2021 Engage Books

Edited by: Alexis Roumanis and Lauren Dick

Text set in Arial Regular.
Chapter headings set in Arial Black.

FIRST EDITION / FIRST PRINTING

LIBRARY AND ARCHIVES CANADA CATALOGUING IN PUBLICATION

Title: The Jurassic period / Ashley Lee.
Names: Lee, Ashley, 1995- author.
Description: Series statement: Dinosaur adventures

Identifiers: Canadiana (print) 20210314737 | Canadiana (ebook) 20210314753
ISBN 978-1-77476-490-9 (hardcover)
ISBN 978-1-77476-491-6 (softcover)
ISBN 978-1-77476-493-0 (pdf)
ISBN 978-1-77476-492-3 (epub)
ISBN 978-1-77476-499-2 (audio)

Subjects:
LCSH: Readers
LCSH: Readers—Dinosaurs.
LCSH: Readers—Paleontology—Jurassic.

Classification: LCC PE1117 .D56 2022C | DDC J428.6—DC23

Contents

What Is the Jurassic Period?

The Jurassic Period is a time in Earth's history when dinosaurs grew to large sizes.

It started about 201 million years ago and ended about 145 million years ago.

What Were Jurassic Dinosaurs?

There were two kinds of Jurassic dinosaurs. Theropods had two legs and ate meat.

Sauropods had long necks and long tails. They had four legs and only ate plants.

What Did Jurassic Dinosaurs Look Like?

Long necks helped Sauropods reach leaves on tall trees.

The legs of sauropods were thick to support their heavy bodies.

Theropods had razor-sharp teeth for tearing meat.

Theropods had short arms with sharp claws at the ends.

9

Where Did Jurassic Dinosaurs Live?

The early Jurassic Period had two large areas of land. They were called Laurasia and Gondwana.

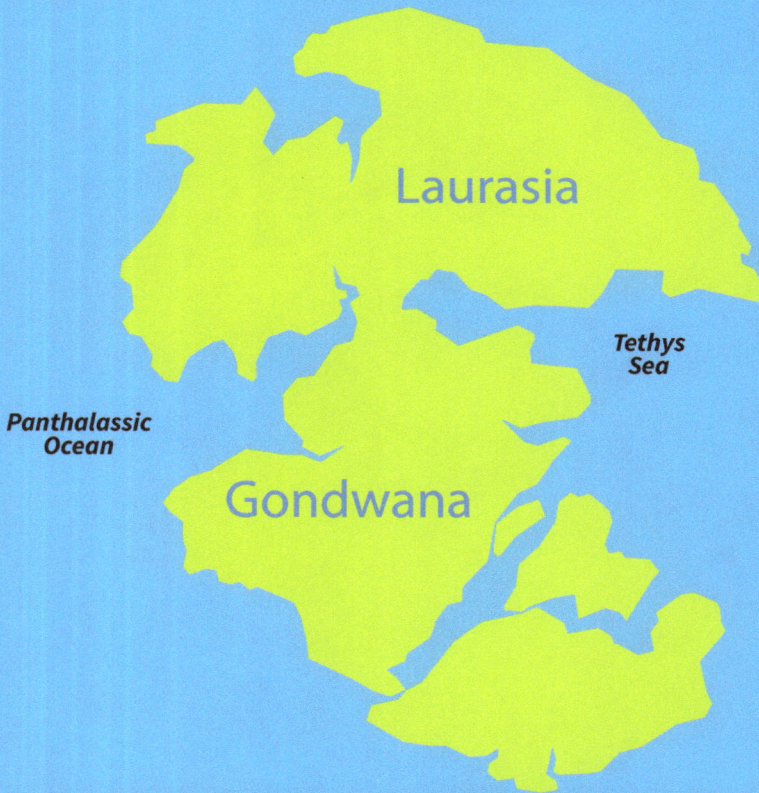

Laurasia

Tethys Sea

Panthalassic Ocean

Gondwana

These began to break into smaller pieces in the late Jurassic Period.

Dinosaurs lived everywhere on Earth in the late Jurassic Period. Camptosaurus (*camp-toe-sore-us*) and diplodocus (*dip-low-dock-us*) lived in the north. Cryolophosaurus (*cry-o-loaf-o-sore-us*) lived in the south.

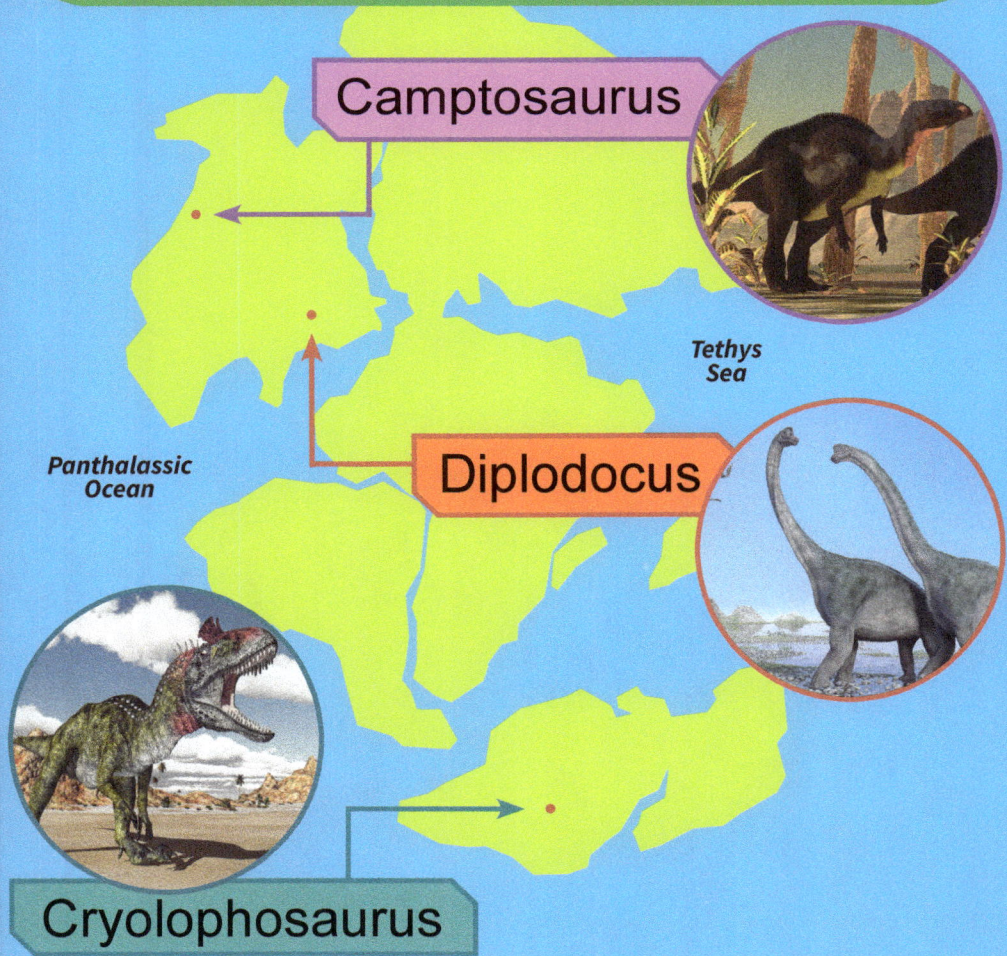

Camptosaurus

Tethys Sea

Panthalassic Ocean

Diplodocus

Cryolophosaurus

	2,000 miles
0	
0	4,000 kilometers (km)

N

Legend
- Land
- Ocean

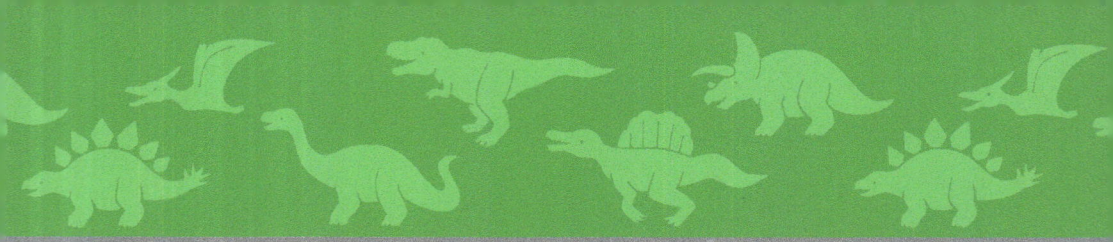

Jurassic Climate

The Jurassic Period had a tropical climate. It was very warm and wet.

The climate helped all plant and animal life to growth. This led to new plants, mammals, and dinosaurs!

Jurassic Plants

There were lots of different plants in the Jurassic Period. They provided food for many dinosaurs.

Today's ferns, horsetails, and club mosses are all plants that were around in the Jurassic Period.

Jurassic Ocean Life

Jurassic oceans were filled with large reptiles. The largest ocean reptiles were plesiosaurs (*plee-see-uh-sores*).

16

Plesiosaurs were some of the first marine reptiles to give birth to babies and not eggs.

Reptiles are cold-blooded animals. They use heat from the sun to stay warm.

Jurassic Flying Creatures

Flying reptiles called pterosaurs (*teh-ruh-sores*) filled Jurassic skies. Pterosaur means winged lizard.

The first pterosaurs were small with long tails. In the late Jurassic Period, pterosaurs grew much larger and had shorter tails.

Kinds of Jurassic Dinosaurs

The back legs of Brachiosaurus (*brae-kee-uh-sore-us*) were shorter than its front legs.

Shunosaurus (*shoon-oh-sore-us*) had spikes on the end of its tail.

Scelidosaurus (*skel-eye-doh-sore-us*) had hard spikes on its body that acted like armor.

Dryosaurus (*dry-oh-sore-us*) had a beak like a bird and leaf-shaped teeth.

Allosaurus (*al-oh-sore-us*) had a weak bite but very sharp teeth for tearing meat.

Compsognathus (*komp-sog-nath-us*) was about the size of a chicken.

Curious Facts About the Jurassic Period

The Jurassic Period was named after the Jura Mountains in Europe.

Giraffatitan (*jih-raff-ah-tie-tan*) is thought to be the tallest dinosaur ever. It was about as tall as an eight-story building.

Sauropods didn't chew their food.

Dinosaurs ate stones to help them mush up the food in their bellies.

Ammonite fossils are some of the most common Jurassic fossils.

Salamanders appeared on Earth for the first time.

How Has the Jurassic Period Impacted the World Today?

Coral reefs began to get bigger and started to become more important in the Jurassic Period. They provided food and shelter for many different kinds of ocean life.

Today, coral reefs block dangerous waves, storms, and floods from hitting coastlines. This protects the people who live there.

What Modern Animals Came From the Jurassic Period?

The dinosaurs that became birds first appeared during the Jurassic Period. They were the first animals on Earth to have feathers.

Archaeopteryx (*aar-kee-aap-tr-uhks*) was one of the first bird-like dinosaurs. Unlike today's birds, they had a full set of teeth.

How Did the Jurassic Period End?

Scientists who study dinosaurs are called paleontologists. They still don't know when the Jurassic Period ended.

Other than a sudden drop in temperature, there are no big clues to mark when the Jurassic Period ended and the Cretaceous Period began.

Quiz

Test your knowledge of the Jurassic Period by answering the following questions. The questions are based on what you have read in this book. The answers are listed on the bottom of the next page.

1 When did the Jurassic Period end?

2 What are the two kinds of Jurassic dinosaurs called?

3 What were the largest ocean reptiles in the Jurassic Period?

4 What does "pterosaur" mean?

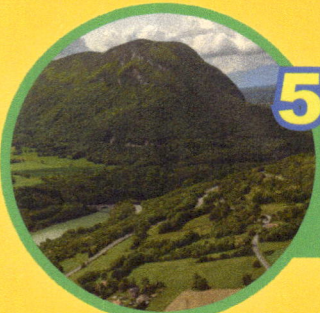

5 What was the Jurassic Period named after?

6 What dinosaur is thought to be the tallest dinosaur ever?

Explore Our Engage Books Readers!

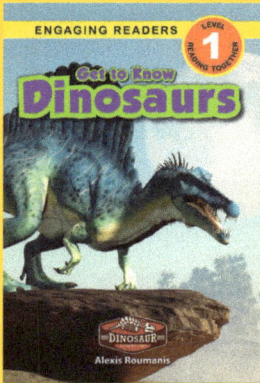

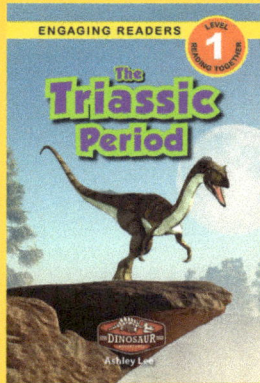

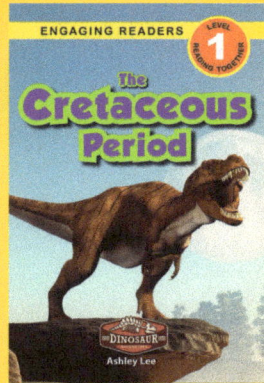

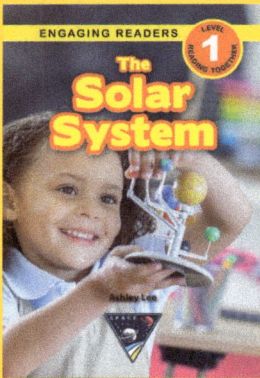

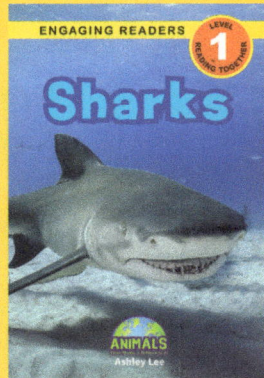

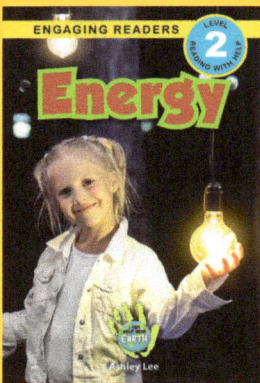

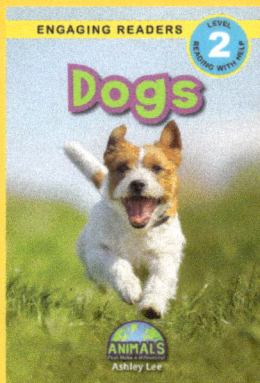

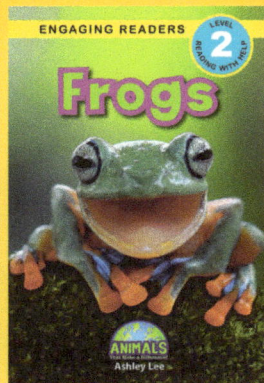

Visit www.engagebooks.com to explore more Engaging Readers.

Answers: 1. About 145 million years ago 2. Theropods and sauropods 3. Plesiosaurs 4. Winged lizard 5. The Jura Mountains 6. Girrafatitan

www.ingramcontent.com/pod-product-compliance
Lightning Source LLC
Chambersburg PA
CBHW051241020426
42331CB00016B/3468